Count by Fives

by Jerry Pallotta
Illustrated by Rob Bolster

Cartwheel
·B·O·O·K·S·®
AN IMPRINT OF
■SCHOLASTIC

New York   Toronto   London   Aukland   Sydney   Mexico City   New Delhi   Hong Kong   Buenos Aires

Thank you to Joan Buffone, W. Dorsey Hammond, Carol Gosset and Denise Gilliland.

——Jerry Pallotta

This book is dedicated to all people who choose to live by the "Golden Rule."

——Rob Bolster

Library of Congress Cataloging-in-Publication Data available.

ISBN 0-439-13520-6

12 11 10 9 8 7 6 5   05 06 07 08 09 10

Printed in U.S.A.   40
First Scholastic printing, January 2000

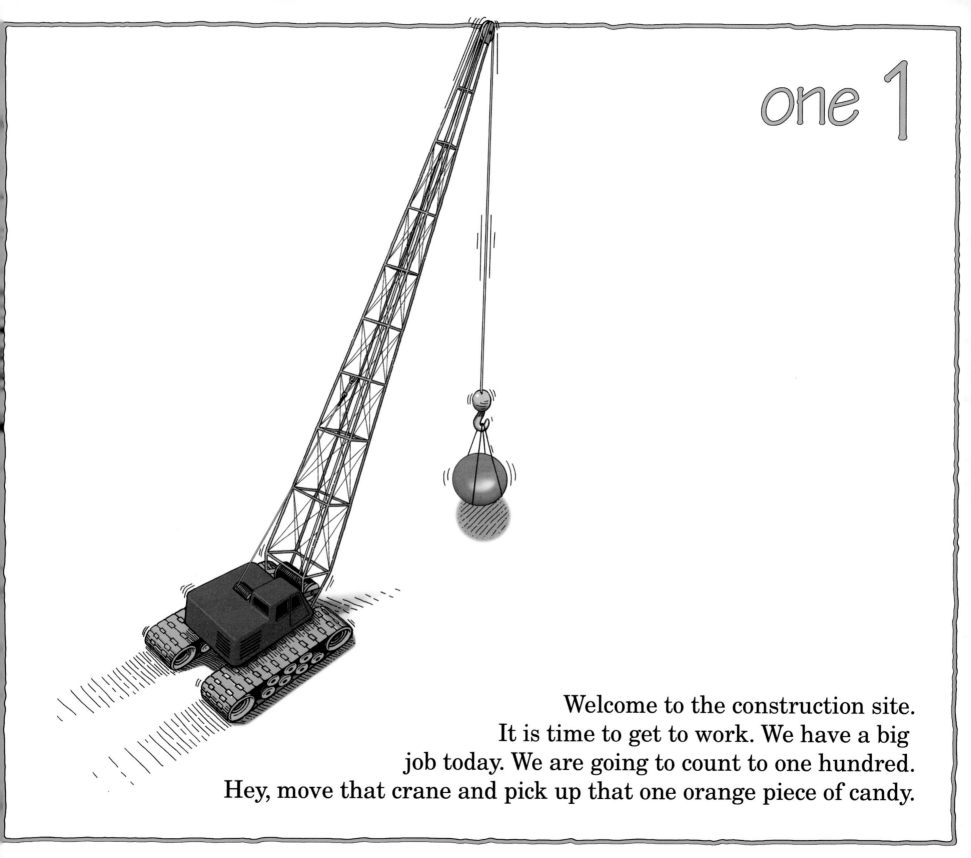

Welcome to the construction site.
It is time to get to work. We have a big
job today. We are going to count to one hundred.
Hey, move that crane and pick up that one orange piece of candy.

2 two

Before we count to one hundred by fives, we are going to count to ten.
The backhoe can pick up the two candies with either its
front bucket or its back bucket.

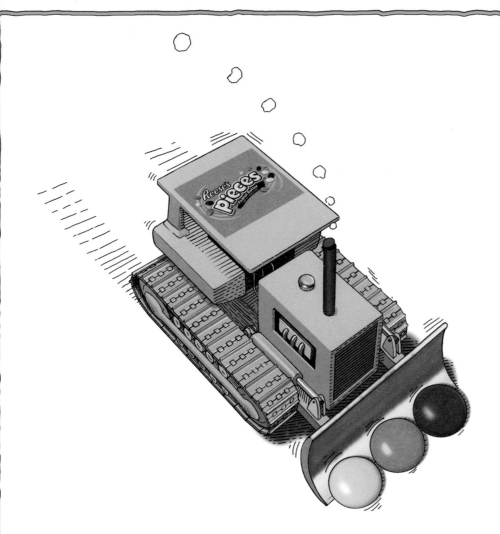

Here comes the bulldozer. Keep on moving the three candies. REESE'S PIECES®
Peanut Butter Candy in a Crunchy Shell comes in three colors:
yellow, orange, and brown.

4 four

Put two pieces in each dump truck.
After you unload those four candies, come back for another load.

Beep. Beep. Beep. Beep. Watch out! That forklift might back up at any time. Be careful while those five candies are being lifted.
Don't run over the pallets.

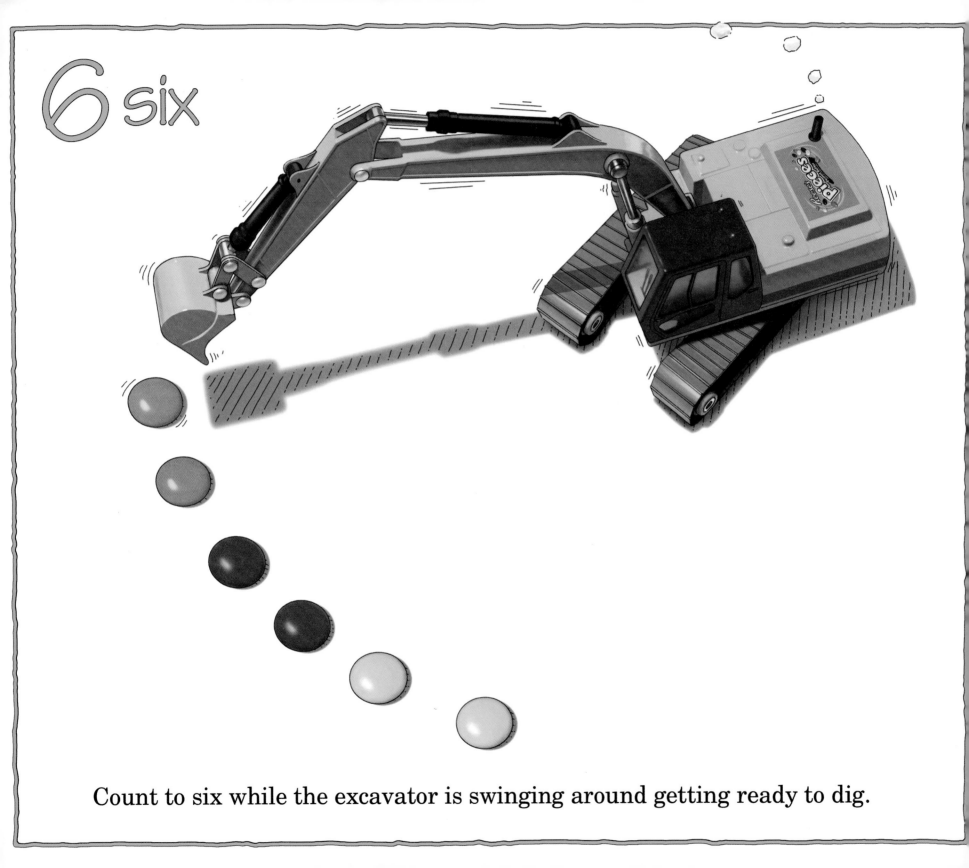

6 six

Count to six while the excavator is swinging around getting ready to dig.

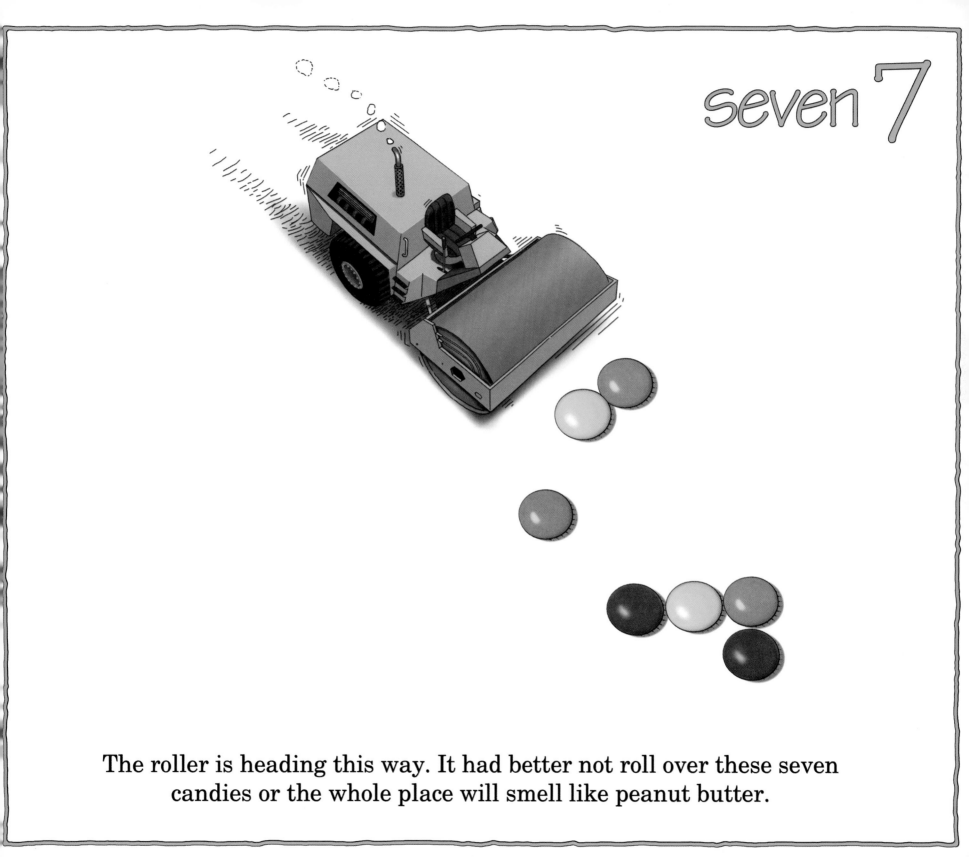

The roller is heading this way. It had better not roll over these seven candies or the whole place will smell like peanut butter.

8 eight

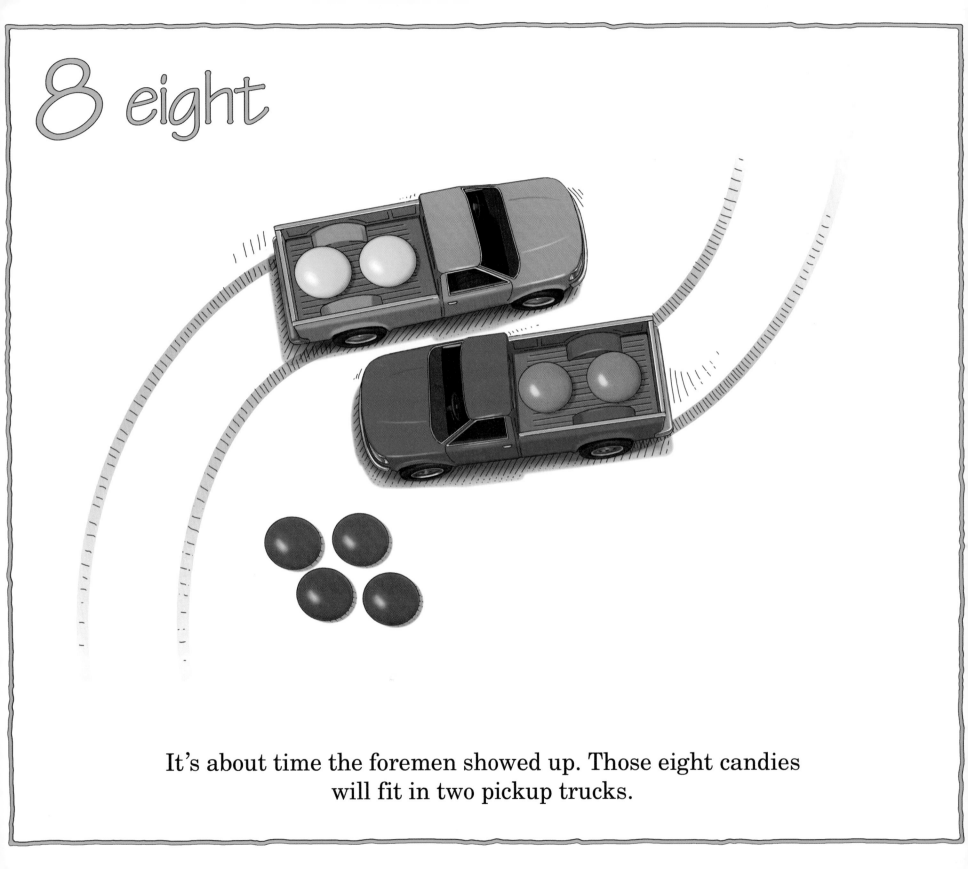

It's about time the foremen showed up. Those eight candies will fit in two pickup trucks.

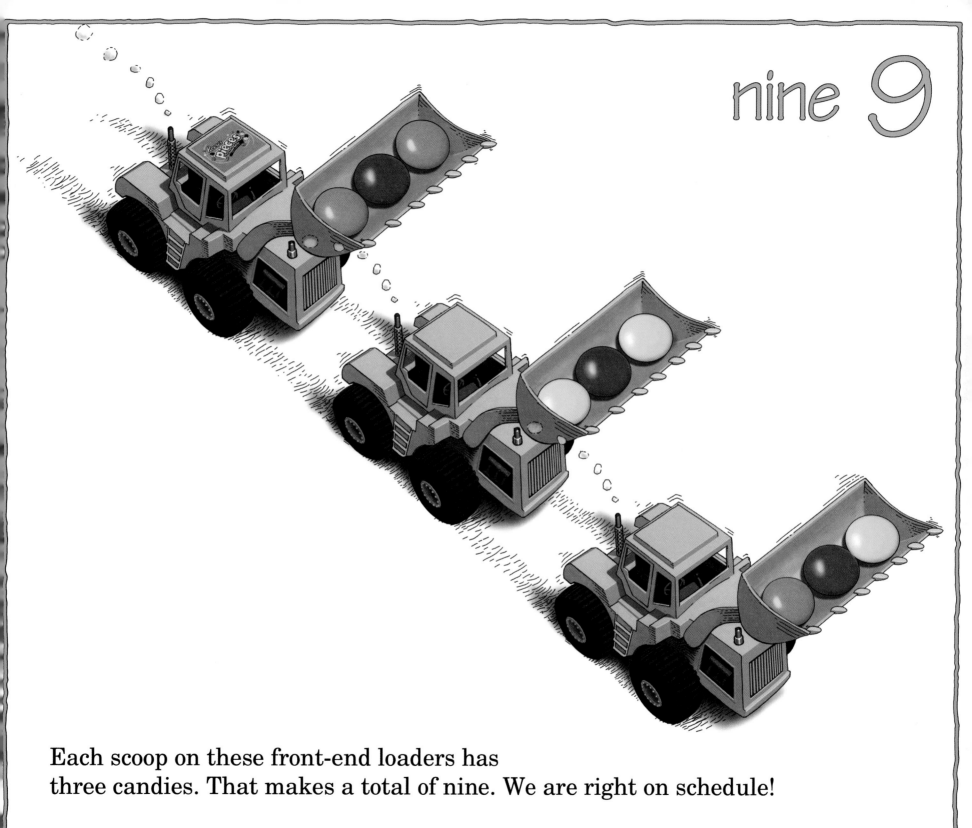

Each scoop on these front-end loaders has
three candies. That makes a total of nine. We are right on schedule!

10 ten

It just rained. Luckily the
ten candies are in the trailer truck, waterproof and safe.
Oh, no! Someone forgot to load them.
We counted to ten by ones, now we are going to count
to one hundred by fives. Five, ten and we keep on going!

This grapple would be better off picking up logs or steel beams but since it is on-site, use it to move the fifteen orange candies.

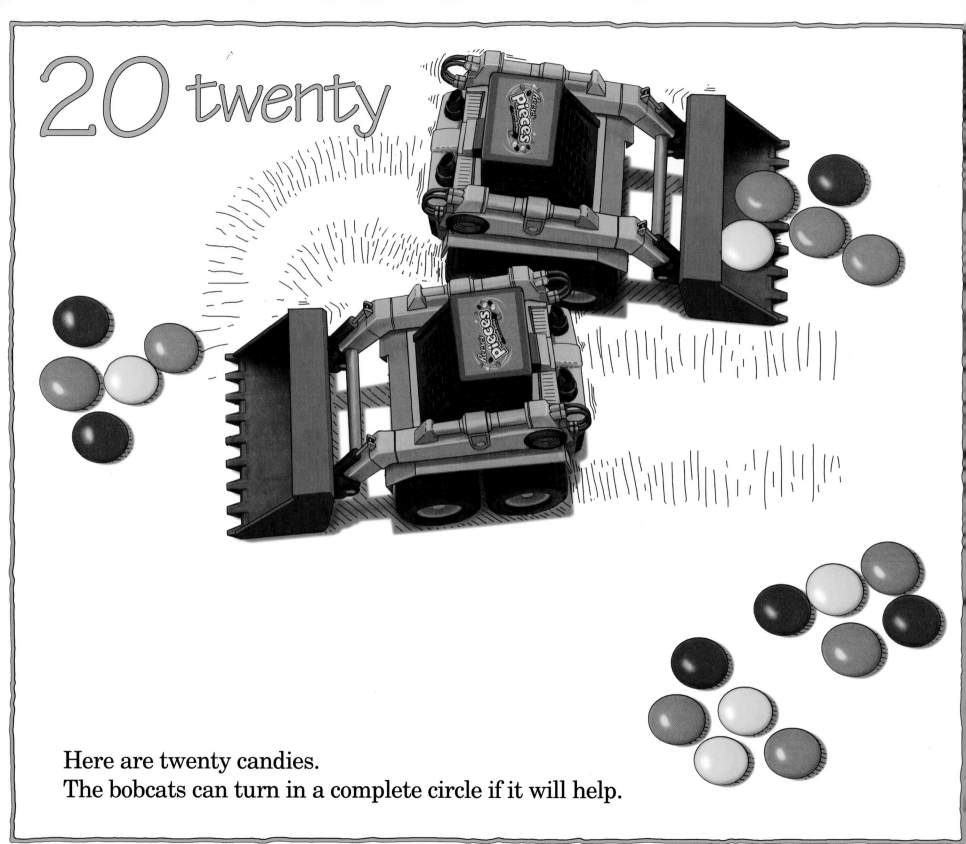

Here are twenty candies.
The bobcats can turn in a complete circle if it will help.

We usually use this rack truck to carry
tools but today we are moving twenty-five candies.

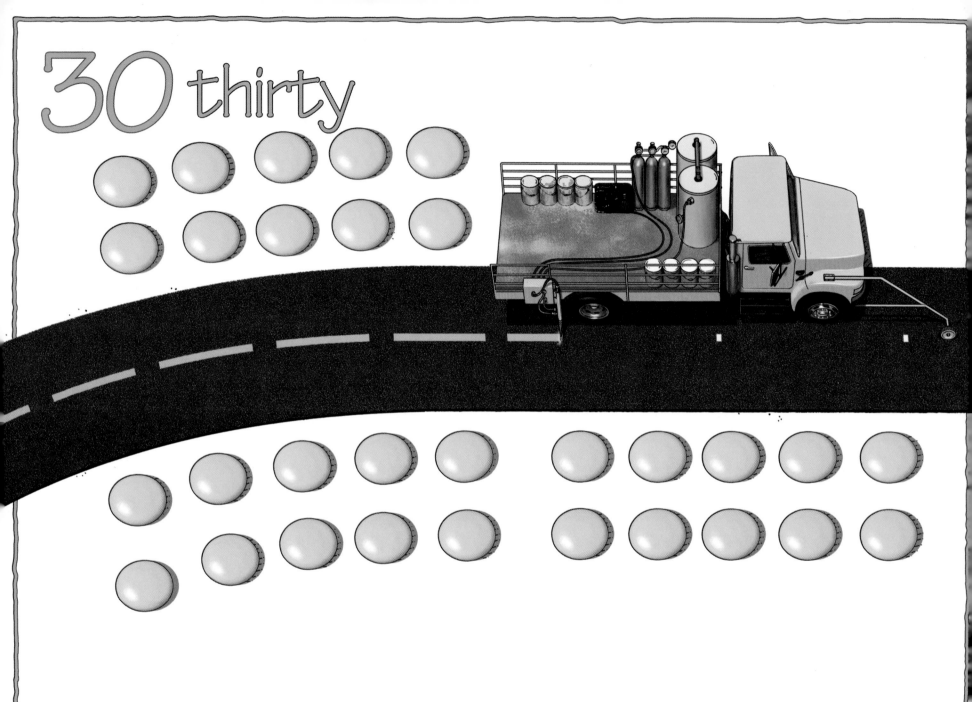

There are thirty yellow candies and a yellow line painting truck painting the yellow lines in the middle of the new road.

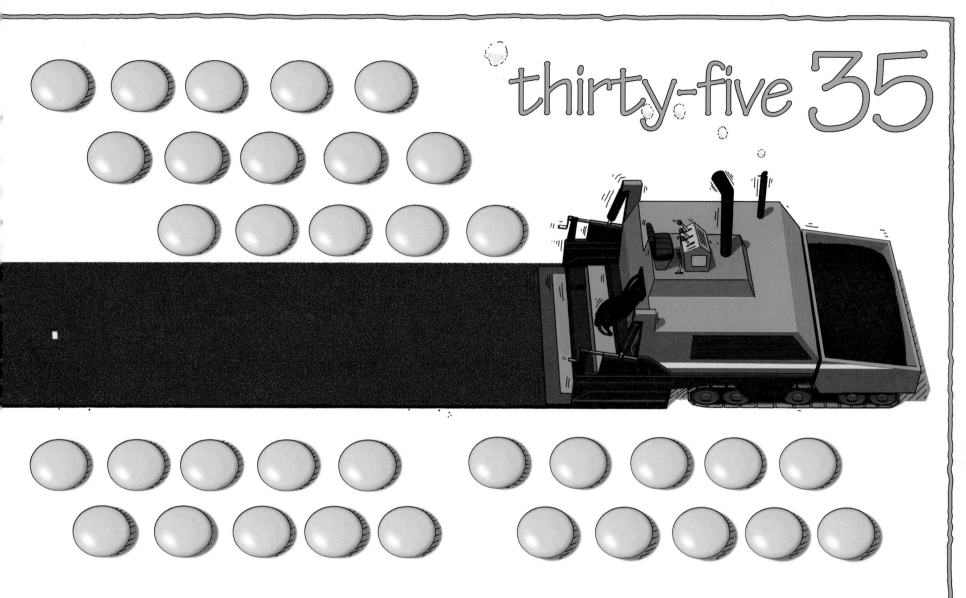

The road paver is laying the asphalt. Count the thirty-five candies
as the road is being built.

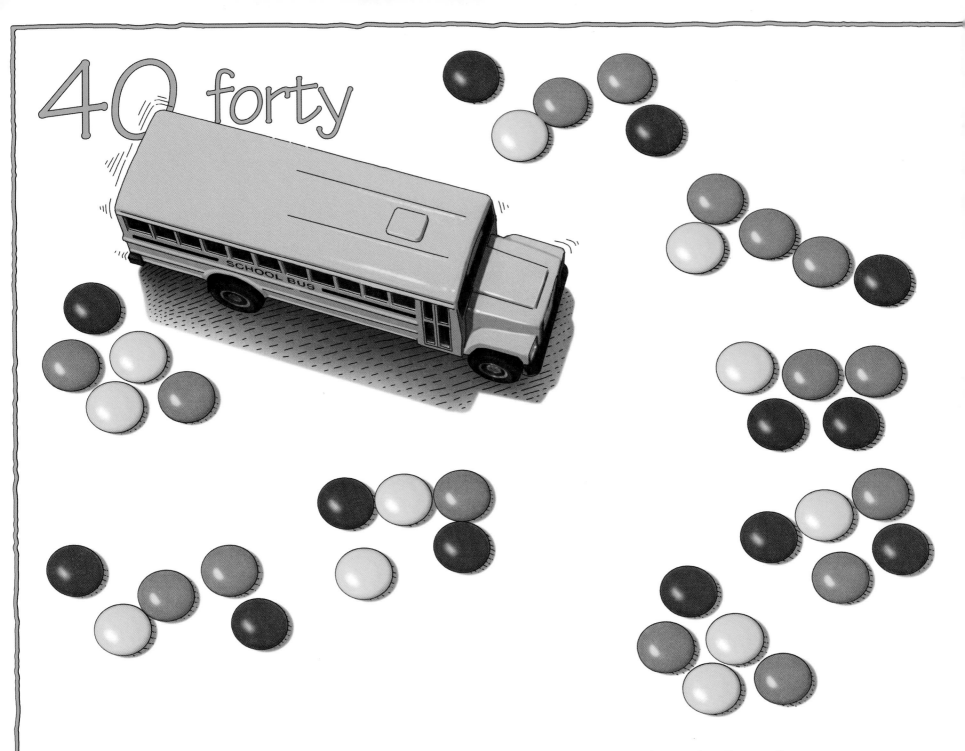

40 forty

Hold the equipment! Stop construction immediately. Let the school bus go by. The kids on the bus can count to forty.

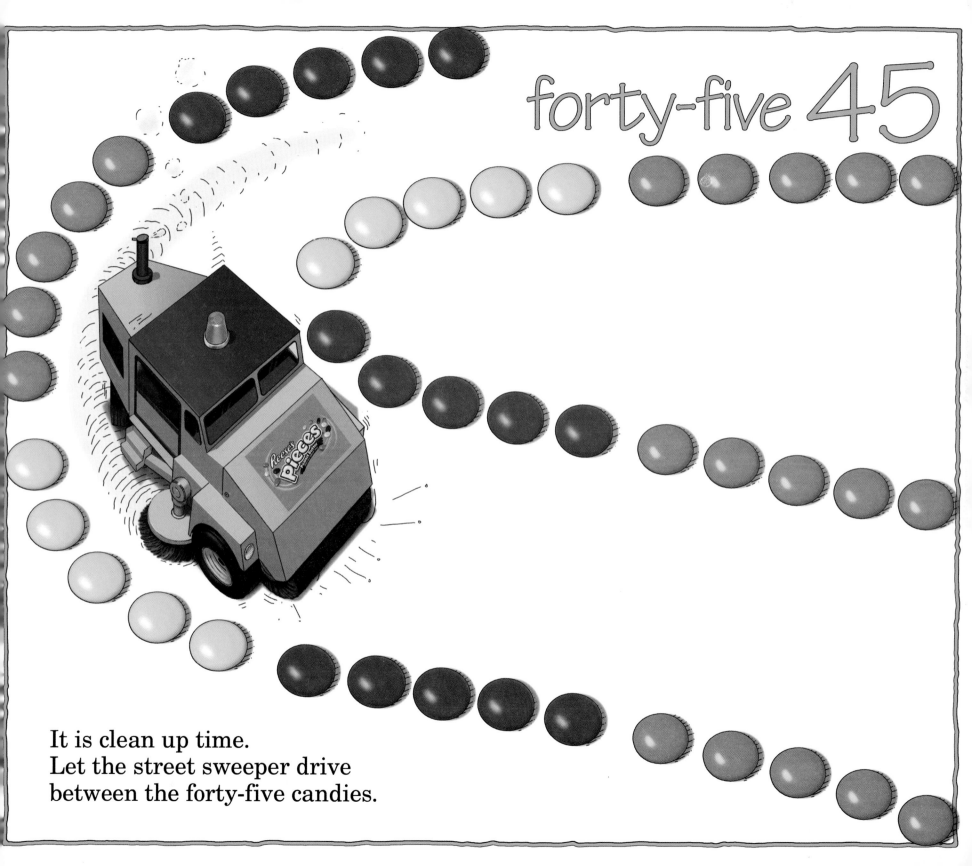

It is clean up time.
Let the street sweeper drive
between the forty-five candies.

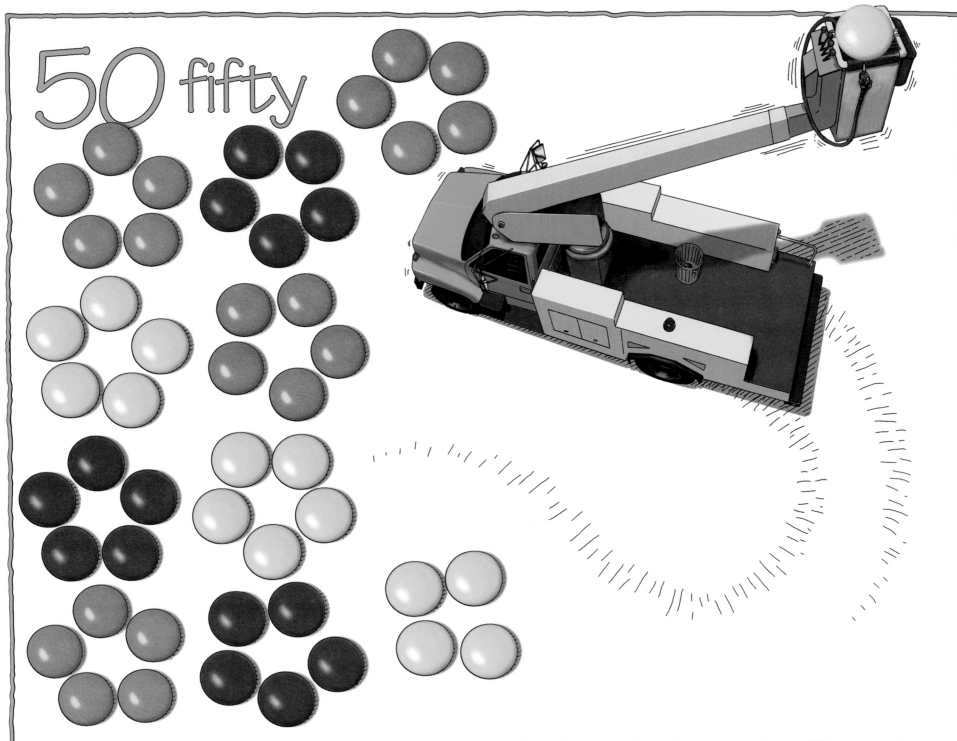

50 fifty

Here are forty-nine candies plus the one in the bucket of the cherry picker. Hooray, that makes fifty pieces of candy! We are halfway to one hundred. The job is looking good.

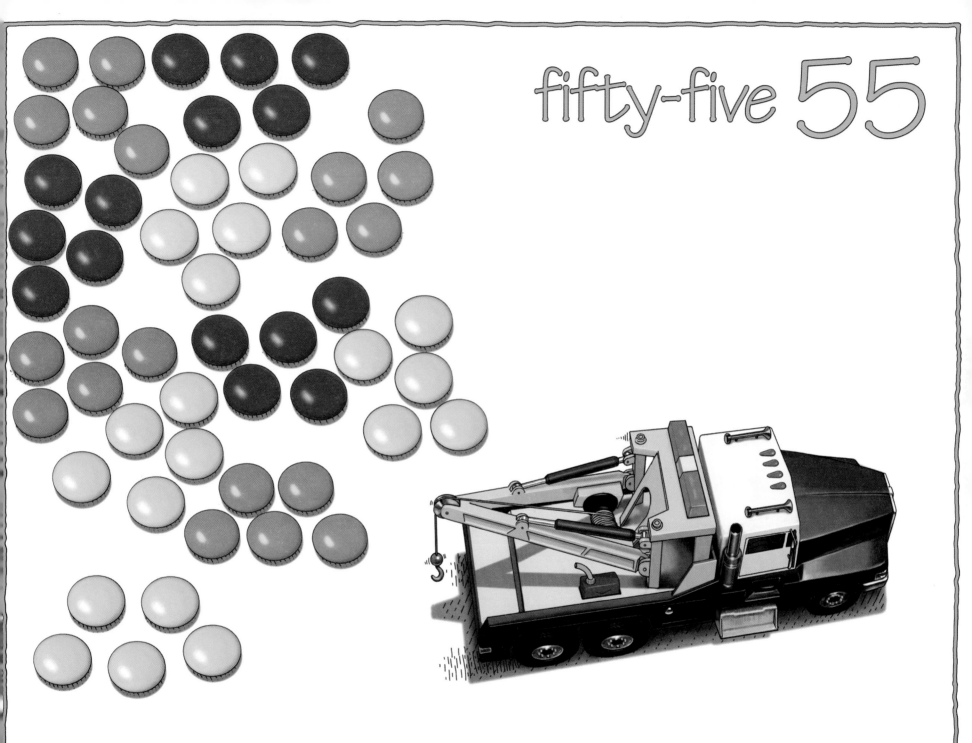

Something broke down. We need a tow truck. We are at fifty-five and counting!

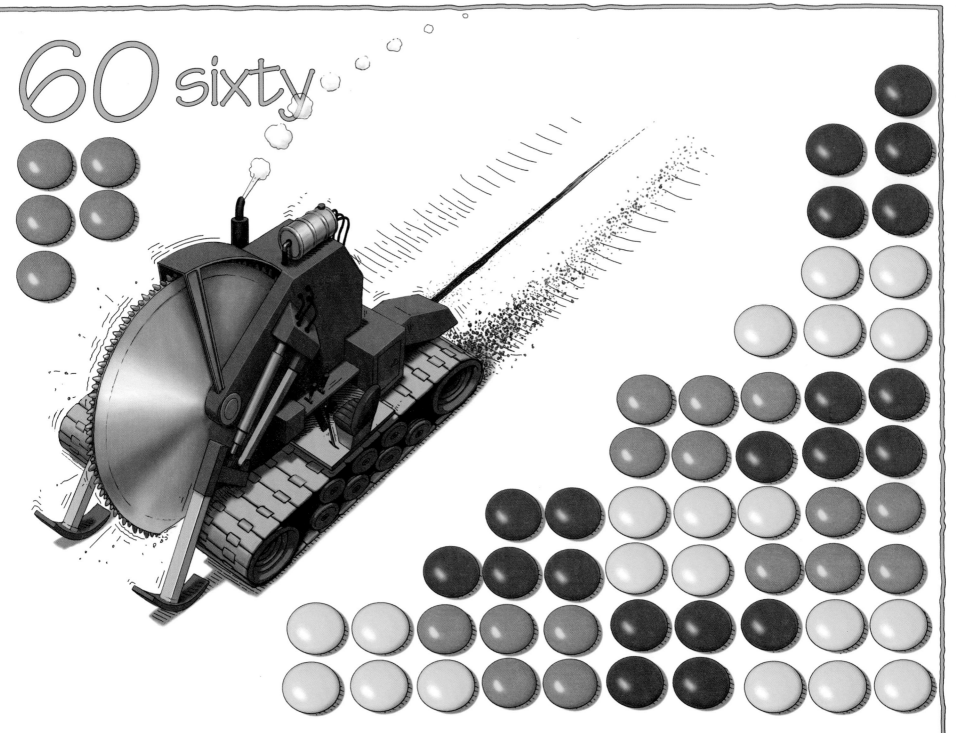

60 sixty

It is time to lay some cable. Caution! Danger! Stand clear
of the road cutter. The road cutter is loud, but we can still count to sixty.

Here is a scissor lift.
It is okay to do some patterning. One yellow,
one orange, one brown, one yellow, one orange, one brown
all the way to sixty-five. One yellow, one orange, one brown. . . .

70 seventy

The tanker truck is finally here. Count the seventy candies and then fill the tank on the pickup. The pickup truck will gas up the other vehicles later.

seventy-five 75

It looks like the cement mixer holds exactly seventy-five candies. Perfect! We are three-quarters of the way to one hundred.

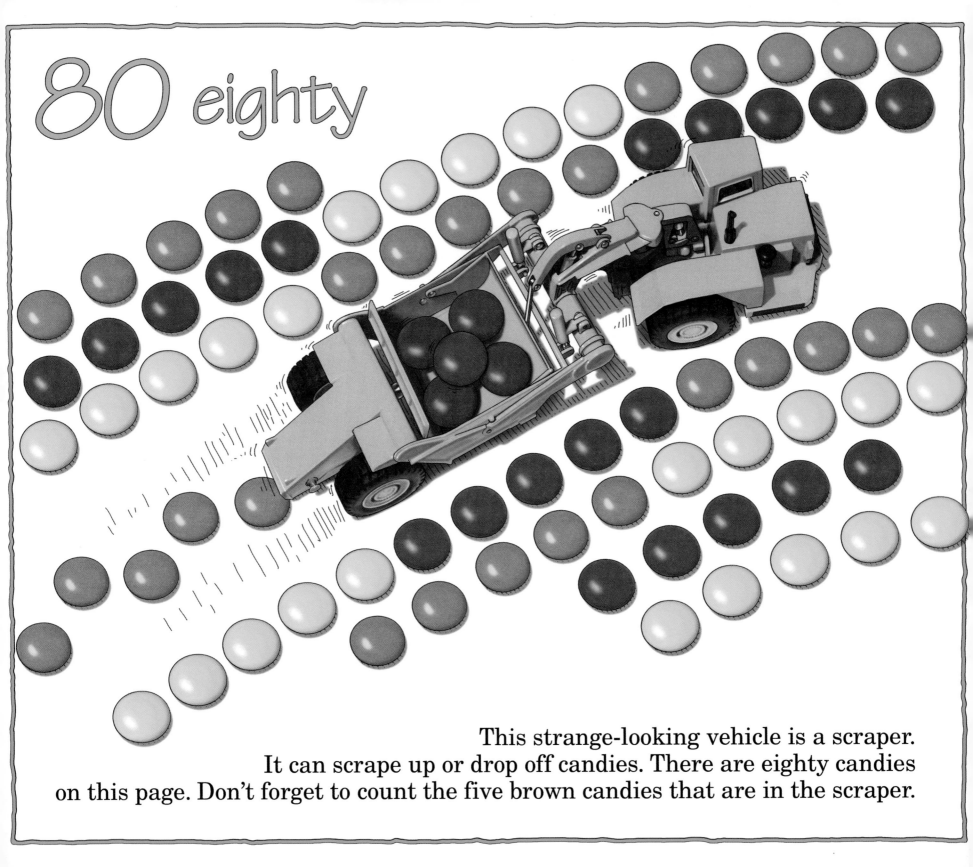

80 eighty

This strange-looking vehicle is a scraper.
It can scrape up or drop off candies. There are eighty candies
on this page. Don't forget to count the five brown candies that are in the scraper.

Here comes the grader right through the eighty-five candies.
In wintertime, the grader can plow snow.

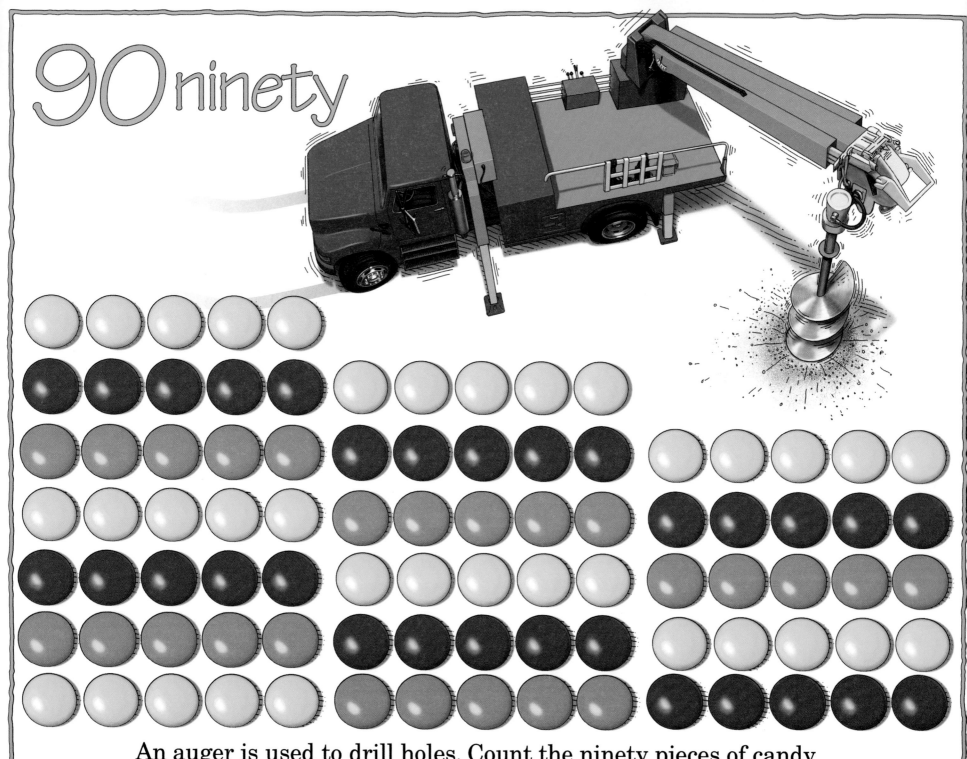

An auger is used to drill holes. Count the ninety pieces of candy
while you are watching the auger drill into the ground.

Here comes a race car! Don't count too fast or you will get a
speeding ticket. Ninety-five candies does not mean ninety-five miles per hour.

one hundred

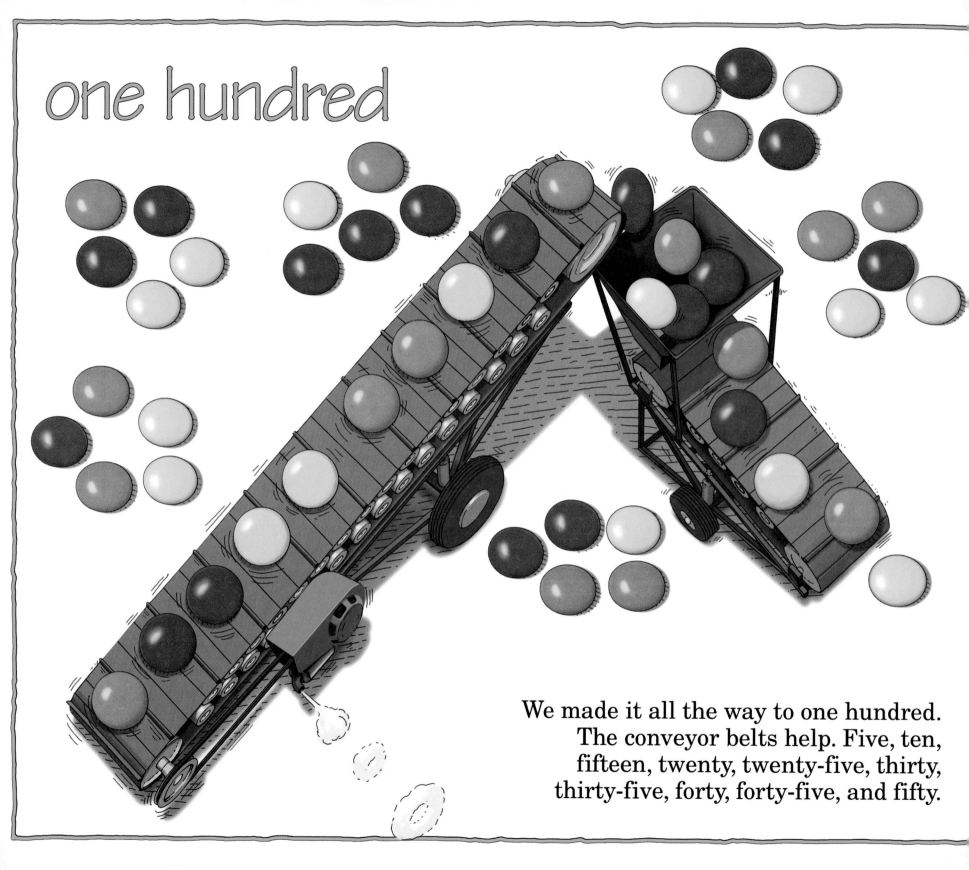

We made it all the way to one hundred. The conveyor belts help. Five, ten, fifteen, twenty, twenty-five, thirty, thirty-five, forty, forty-five, and fifty.

100

And keep on counting: Fifty-five, sixty,
sixty-five, seventy, seventy-five, eighty, eighty-five,
ninety, ninety-five, ONE HUNDRED! Someone left the
compressor and jackhammers on the ground. Is it time for a snack?

O zero

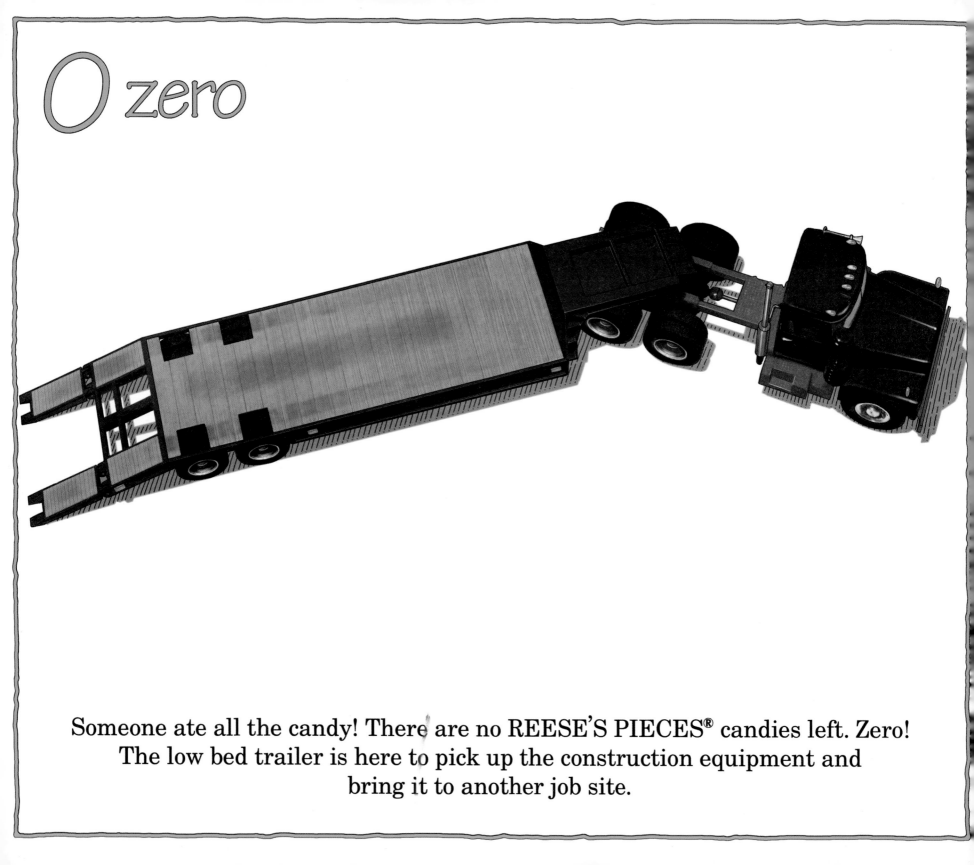

Someone ate all the candy! There are no REESE'S PIECES® candies left. Zero!
The low bed trailer is here to pick up the construction equipment and
bring it to another job site.